BEFORE YOU LEAVE THE

LOCKER
ROOM

BEFORE YOU LEAVE THE
LOCKER ROOM

Pre-Game Devotions for Athletes

LEE SHEPPARD

Before You Leave the Locker Room:
Pre-Game Devotions for Athletes
by Lee Sheppard

Cover Design by Mike Hadden

© Copyright 2013

ST. PAUL PRESS, DALLAS, TEXAS

First Printing, 2013

All Scripture used is from the New American Standard Version of the Bible.

ISBN-10: 0-9849441-4-1
ISBN-13: 978-0-9849441-4-9

Printed in the U.S.A.

To Coach Rodney Walker.
Congratulations on winning over 300 games.

CONTENTS

ACKNOWLEDGEMENTS

In the fall of 2010 I became the Chaplain of the Mary Persons High School Football Team. There are many aspects of this opportunity that have made this a unique experience for me. Perhaps the most gripping of those, however, are the relationships that have been forged over the past four years.

This experience has changed my life in many ways, not the least of which has been the opportunity to invest in the lives of a special group of athletes. I can honestly say that I have had the privilege of working with some of the finest coaches and young men anywhere.

I want to thank my Lord and Savior Jesus Christ who has changed my life and given me the passion for this ministry.

I would also like to thank two groups of people who

have continued to support me along the way. Encouragers comprise the first group. These are the people who have encouraged me to pursue this ministry opportunity. Although, there have been many encouragers, special thanks must go to Bob Bumgarner, Mabel White Baptist Church, Haskell Dunn, and Rick Lucas.

Enablers make up the second group. They are the Mary Persons coaching staff and my team at Mabel White. I want to thank Coach Rodney Walker for giving me this opportunity initially; and also to Coach Brian Nelson for keeping me in this position. Your trust has meant the world to me and I do not take it for granted. Also, I want to thank my good friend, Mike Hadden, my Communications Director, for helping to put this project together, carry the workload and perform so professionally.

Finally, I give thanks for my family. Gina, you have been the ultimate supportive wife. God knew what He was doing when He put us together over thirty years ago. I could not have found a better partner anywhere. I love you and thank you for the fact that you always serve beside me as "one also called." Your support is without question the reason I have gone this far in the journey. Matthew, Megan, and Micah, your dad loves you. I am so proud of each of you and can't wait to see what God is going to do in your lives in the years to come.

INTRODUCTION

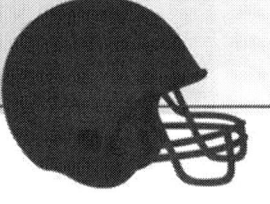

Higher School Football — there's nothing like it! When the seasons begin to change and fall is in the air it's time for football. In the south, football is a cultural thing. It seems like the whole climate of towns and cities are influenced by it. There is nothing like Friday night. The stadium is full, the crowd is loud, the players are excited, the coaches are focused, and you can just feel the electricity in the air. To this day I still get a shot of adrenaline as I anticipate kickoff. It's time to buckle up, focus, and get after it!

For several years I've had the privilege of being the Chaplain of the Mary Persons Bulldogs football team in Forsyth, Georgia. The program is known throughout the state as a winning program. Dan Pitts and Rodney Walker have helped build it into what it has become today. In fact, they are two of the winningest coaches in GHSA history; each eclipsing the 300-win mark. As Chaplain I have been given an insider's perspective of *Bulldog football*. This has been one of the most rewarding experiences of my life. I have thoroughly enjoyed interacting with the players and coaches. I have built relationships that will last for a lifetime.

My primary responsibility as Chaplain has been to come alongside the coaches and parents and give encouragement, counsel, and a biblical perspective on life issues. Each week I give a pre-game devotion. I choose a "word for the week" that the players and coaches can apply to life on and off the field. These devotions challenge them to be all that God wants them to be. They are affirmations that they are doing the right thing. And they are instruction on how to get even better.

I have a God-given passion to invest in the lives of young men. I've asked God to allow me to personally mentor over 100 men in my lifetime to be all that God wants them to be. Although I haven't reached that goal just yet, I am diligently working toward it. The time that I get to spend with these young athletes is very valuable and I don't take it lightly. I realize that this ministry is a privilege and not a right. This is a huge opportunity to shape the values, thinking, and faith of future husbands, fathers, and leaders and

I have asked God for His help and direction.

This book is a compilation of some of the pre-game talks—devotions, if you will—I have given over the years. I hope as you read them you are challenged to be all that God wants you to be, encouraged in the things you are doing right, and that you will find some instruction that will make you even better. These talks were originally shared in the context of football, so the application is often related to the team or the game. However, because God's principles are true and always consistent, you can gain nuggets of truth that can inspire and instruct regardless of the sport you are playing.

It is my prayer that these talks will be an encouragement to you in your faith journey.

Lee Sheppard
Chaplain
Mary Persons Bulldogs
1 John 5:14-15

UNITY

One of the greatest teams in sports history was the 1980 United States Hockey Team. Going into the Lake Placid Olympics no one thought that the US would contend for a gold medal. Their roster was made up of collegiate players with only one returning player from the 1976 Olympic Team. Compared to some of the other teams in the Olympics, the Americans were truly a long shot.

The Russians on the other hand, were the heavy favorite. Their players were seasoned on the ice and trained in world class facilities. Their life was hockey. They won almost every World Championship and Olympic Tournament since 1954. In fact, in exhibitions leading up to the Olympics they touted a

5-3-1 record against teams in the National Hockey League; and the year before they routed the National Hockey League All Stars 6-0 in the Challenge Cup. The Russians play, along with the Cold War, made them rivals with United States. However, it was almost a foregone conclusion that Russia would take the gold.

As the tournament progressed, the Americans were surprising. Their performance was physical and they showed themselves as a very cohesive team. They worked hard for their wins and were forced to play their starters the whole time. The Russians, on the other hand, were defeating their opponents with lopsided victories and were resting their best players as they readied themselves for the medal rounds. Both teams excelled and were on a collision course for the semi-finals.

On February 22, 1980, the United States and the Russians met in the semi-finals. With a packed field house and the crowd waving American Flags, the atmosphere was electric. The United States had overachieved. They had come together and done what no one thought they could do. In fact, the day before the semi-final match, columnist Dave Anderson wrote in *The New York Times*, "Unless the ice melts, or unless the United States team or another team performs a miracle, the Russians are expected to easily win the Olympic gold medal for the sixth time in the last seven tournaments."

As the match began it was war on ice. Both teams battled with everything they had. The momentum ebbed and flowed. Finally, with the game tied and only ten minutes left in the match, U.S. team captain Mike Eruzione fired a shot past the Russian defender Myshkin putting the United States ahead 4-3. For the first time in the match the Russians were behind and they attacked. With each attack they were turned back by the stingy American defenders. With just under one minute on the clock, the Russians made a last gasp when Vladimir Petrov's shot went wide. The United States controlled the puck and "the miracle on ice" actually happened!

The key for the 1980 United States Hockey team was their unity.

In fact, the key to *any* great team is unity. Unity is the cord that binds a team together. A team consists of different people with different views, beliefs, personalities, strengths, and weaknesses. At first glance you may think these differences look like weaknesses. In fact, diversity without unity is a recipe for disaster. However, diversity can really be an asset when the team is unified. Team unity is when the team has a singular focus, purpose, and goal.

UNITY. It's the key to a winning season. Will you come together as a team and coaches and work toward the same goal?

King David, in the Bible, had some insight into this whole aspect we call unity.

"Behold, how good and how pleasant it is for brothers to dwell together in unity! It is like the precious oil upon the head, coming down upon the beard, even Aaron's beard, coming down upon the edge of his robes. It is like the dew of Hermon coming down upon the mountains of Zion; For there the Lord commanded the blessing—life forever." Psalm 133:1-3 (NASB)

In Old Testament days whenever they anointed someone with oil, they poured the oil over the head and it soaked the entire body. This is a great picture of how unity affects us.

Unity Affects the Way You Think

As Coach Lou Holtz said, "Winners and losers are not born; they are the product of how they think." If you think you're a winner your chances of winning increase, but if you think you're a loser your chances of losing increase.

What do you believe about yourself? What do you believe about each other? When you come together in unity it will have a direct bearing on how you think and will impact your team.

Unity Affects the Effort You Make

When the priest poured the oil over the head of a person, it covered his head but it also covered his chest or his heart. Unity affects the effort you give.

Think about your own team. You know you've worked hard. You've put in the extra hours. You've paid the price with early morning workouts, matt drills, and summer camp in over 100 degree heat. All of your blood, sweat, and tears have been focused on the game. You're in shape, you've done the work and now it is time to take care of business.

> *"I can't believe God put us on the earth to be ordinary."*
>
> *Lou Holtz*

Lou Holtz says, "I can't believe God put us on the

earth to be ordinary." Your team is made up of a bunch of extraordinary people. Think about it— you are one of a kind. You are God's masterpiece. The Bible says you are fearfully and wonderfully made. There is no one else like you. You have different gifts, skills, and abilities. Some of you are fast, some of you are strong, and some of you are fast *and* strong. If you will come together in unity as brothers and harness your God-given gifts and abilities there is no limit to how far you can go. You've got all the talent and ability you need to accomplish your goals.

Unity Affects the Way You Play

Have you ever tried to walk around in wet blue jeans? It doesn't feel right does it? You walk differently. When the priest anointed someone with oil it covered the head, ran down over the heart, and eventually made its way down to the hem of the garment.

Unity has a direct impact on the way you play the game and the way you live your life. Remember this life lesson *"Tough times pass, tough people last."*

Whether it's a football game or life, there will be adversity. Things are not going to go your way all the time. You're not going to get all the breaks. You will make some mistakes. You will blow an assignment.

But just remember, *"Tough times pass, tough people last."* If you will stick together and be united in a common goal—the results will be really, really good!

BOW YOUR HEAD

Dear God,

I thank You for the other athletes on my team and for our coaches. Thank You that we've all been willing to put in the effort, the practice and the planning for our next game.

I pray that You will bring all of our gifts, abilities, talents and personalities together in unity. Help us believe in each other, to give our very best effort, and to play in such a way that it is evident that we are one.

In Jesus' Name, Amen.

COURAGE

When you think about courage there are many players in the history of the NFL who could qualify to be the most courageous player. However, many believe that Brian Piccolo is probably the most courageous player in the history of the NFL.

Though he was not drafted in the 1965 NFL draft, Piccolo tried out for the Chicago Bears as a free agent and made the practice team. In 1966, he made the roster and played primarily on special teams. The next year he became the back-up tailback to Gail Sayers and in 1969, he became the starting fullback.

In November 1969, during one of the worst seasons

in Chicago Bears history, Piccolo took himself out of the ninth game against Atlanta complaining of chest pains. After a medical examination it was determined that he had a tumor in his lungs. In June 1970, Brian Piccolo died. In May, just a month before Piccolo's death, Gail Sayers accepted the NFL's most courageous player award. However, when he came to the platform to accept the award he told the crowd that they had chosen the wrong man for this award. Sayers went on to say, "I love Brian Piccolo, and I'd like all of you to love him, too. When you hit your knees to pray tonight, please ask God to love him."

COURAGE. Winston Churchill said, "Courage is the first of human qualities because it is the quality which guarantees all others."

- Courage is an issue of the heart.
- It is what separates those who excel and those who don't.
- It means standing on your convictions.
- It is performing with conviction and passion.
- It is continuing to get up every time you get knocked down.
- It is doing the right thing, even when it's not easy.
- It is battling to accomplish your goals.
- It is finishing what you start.

In the Bible there is a man who is the picture of what courage **IS NOT**. His name was Jonah, a prophet whom God was sending to the wicked city of Nineveh.

*"Arise, go to Nineveh the great city and cry against it, for their wickedness has come up before Me... But Jonah arose to flee to Tarshish from the presence of the LORD."*Jonah 1:1, 3 (NASB)

If you read the whole story in the Bible you'll notice a pattern that begins to emerge. He went down to Joppa, down into the bottom of a ship, down into the belly of the fish. He went down, down, down! That's what a lack of courage does. When you retreat you're going down!

> *"Courage is the first of human qualities because it is the quality which guarantees all others."*
>
> *Winston Churchill*

Here are three things that retreat will do for you:

Retreat Reveals Our Fear

God told Jonah to go to Nineveh and he ran in the opposite direction to Tarshish. Jonah's disobedience was rooted in fear. Maybe he was afraid of what would happen if he *did* go. Maybe he was afraid of what God would ask him to do. Maybe he was afraid he would fail. Maybe he was afraid he would succeed. So instead of doing what he was supposed to do, he ran from the challenge that was in front of him.

There are going to be times when challenges present themselves to you. There will be times when there is something so big that you are afraid of what might happen. There may be times when the opportunity of a lifetime presents itself. Remember this, "Never Retreat!" Stand your ground and be courageous!

Retreat Results In Adversity

So Jonah runs away from God's plan for his life. Remember this, God has a plan for your life. He has numbered your days and knows how long you'll live. He knows the challenges you face now and the opportunities that will present themselves in the future. Jonah gets on a ship and retreats from the challenge. The result was adversity.

First, there was a storm. All of a sudden the wind began to blow and the waves began to crash on the side of the boat to the point that they thought the boat would sink. Here's the principle: *nothing good comes from retreating or running from a challenge.* Life will get bumpy and you will realize that what you are going through is a result of your decision to retreat. You can only blame yourself when this happens.

Second, there was a fish. The other passengers on the boat realized that Jonah was the problem and they threw him out of the boat and a huge fish came and swallowed him. For three days he was in the belly of that fish. Here's another principle: *When you are running from something it will be apparent to others, and you will be swallowed up by the situation.*

You see, retreat seems like the easy way, but really it is not. It takes courage to stay in the fight, stand your ground and finish what you start. When you demonstrate courage it puts your character, or lack of character, on full display.

Retreat Results In Remorse

Read what Jonah said in verse 2: *"I called out of my distress to the LORD, and He answered me. I cried for help from the depth of Sheol; You heard my voice."* When you run from opportunity there is always remorse.

At this point Jonah is in the belly of the fish. He'd been sloshing around for three days and finally he called out to God for help. I'm sure he said, "If I could just do it over again! If I could just have one more chance!" If you read the whole story you'll discover that in this case, he got that chance. However, it doesn't always work out that way. Sometimes the decisions we make cost us in a big way.

Courage is an interesting thing. Sometimes it is big and grandiose. However, often it is small and unnoticeable to the average onlooker. Courage is not the absence of fear, but the ability to keep breathing and walking *through* the fear.

Life sometimes forces you to make tough choices. You can run and hide, or you can stand up and deal with reality. When you stand your ground and deal with what is coming, you are being courageous whether you realize it or not.

Remember these four things when you want to be courageous on the field:

- **Be willing to do what is difficult.** Some of the best things in life are not easy, but do them anyway.

- **Watch how you talk to yourself.** If you tell

yourself you can't—you won't. "Can't" never accomplishes anything.

- **Remember the small things.** Many times attention to the small things will make the difference.

- **Just do it.** You're in the fight so you might as well win it. A lot of times there is a fine line between success and failure.

Be Courageous—Never Retreat!

BOW YOUR HEAD

Dear God,

Help me be courageous in all that I do. I pray that I will stand up for what is right and be willing to obey You regardless of the cost.

In Jesus' Name, Amen.

EXECUTE

Who would you say had the best offense in the history of the NFL? Drew Brees, quarterback for the New Orleans Saints, led the most explosive offense in the NFL in 2012 to a 13-3 record and an NFC South title. Brees broke Dan Marino's passing record, throwing for 5,476 yards and 46 touchdowns. Brees also set NFL records for most completions in a season with 468, most 300-plus yard passing games in a season with 13, most 350-plus yard passing games with four, and a 71.2 percent completion percentage.

The key to this success was that he executed at a very high level.

Here are some keys to great execution:

- **You have to know your team.** This creates chemistry.

- **You have to set clear goals.** In other words, everyone understands what the target is.

- **You have to follow through.** It's not enough to talk about it, you've got to go and do it.

- **You have to listen to your coaches.** If you don't listen to your coaches you'll never execute at a high level.

- **You have to know yourself.** You've got to learn what you are willing to do, as well as what you can and will do.

EXECUTE. In the book of Joshua there is a great example of execution. The Children of Israel were coming out of the wilderness where they had wandered for 40 years and were about to enter the Promised Land. They already knew there were fortified cities and giants in the land. They knew they would be challenged, but God had promised them that every place they stepped belonged to them. They knew if they executed God's plan they would be fine. So they expected to win; they expected victory.

Here are three things that are involved in good execution:

A Worthy Opponent

Jericho was the most fortified city in the Promised Land. Its armies were barricaded behind walls that were 25 feet tall and six feet wide. To say the least, the army of Israel had its hands full. Looking at the city from the outside, the prospect of victory didn't look very good. Jericho was a worthy opponent and their reputation preceded them. Just 40 years before, 12 spies had been sent to spy out the land. They came back with the report that the cities were fortified and there were giants in the land.

In spite of this worthy opponent, Israel marched forward because they had been given a promise from God in Joshua 1:3, *"Every place on which the sole of your foot treads, I have given it to you."*

You have a worthy opponent every time you take the field. They are big, fast, talented and tenacious. On paper and film they look pretty good. However, just because something looks a certain way doesn't mean that's the way it is. Just because someone looks hard to beat doesn't mean they can't be beaten.

Think of these similarities:

- You've got them on their field—Israel fought the battle of Jericho on their field.

- You've got a talented opponent—Israel had a talented opponent. Jericho had not been defeated.

- You've got to travel—Israel had to travel.

- Some might say that you are rebuilding—Israel was rebuilding. They had spent 40 years in the wilderness.

Yes, you've got a worthy opponent, but it's going to be a great game. If you can't get up for the game, you just can't get up!

A Workable Plan

Every team that executes at a high level has a workable plan. Israel had a plan. For six days they were to march around the outside of the city. The priests blew their trumpets as they marched around the city with the Ark of the Covenant, preceded and followed by the army. They marched in silence. No one said a word for six days, just as Joshua had instructed them. They executed their plan flawlessly.

Likewise, you've worked on a plan. The opponent has been studied and now it's time to execute the plan. You know your team, you have a clear goal, and you've listened to the coaches' instructions. You have followed through and you know yourself. Everything is in place for you to execute the plan.

A Winning Attitude

When you read this account, the thing that is striking is that Israel had a winning attitude. They expected to win. Losing was not in their thinking. The result?

- **They executed with courage.** They faced their opponent head-to-head.

- **They executed with confidence.** They believed in the plan.

- **They executed with conviction**. They were in it to win it.

They believed they were going to win and they won.

On the seventh day the priests and the army, along with the Ark of the Covenant, marched around the walls seven times. And on the seventh time around:

"So the people shouted, and priests blew the trumpets; and when the people heard the sound of the trumpet, the people shouted with a great shout and the wall fell down flat, so that the people went up into the city, every man straight ahead, and they took the city." (Joshua 6:20, NASB)

You see, when you execute as you have been instructed the unbelievable becomes believable, the unbeatable becomes beatable, and the impossible becomes possible. Israel believed they would win and they won! They won because they executed.

You've got a great opportunity when you play. You have a worthy opponent. You have a workable plan. Here's the question: Will you have a winning attitude? Take the challenge to go and execute.

- **Execute with courage**—don't be intimidated. Go head-to-head with them.

- **Execute with confidence**—you have the plan and the talent to accomplish your goal.

- **Execute with conviction**—give it everything

you've got for 48 minutes.

Be in it to win it!

BOW YOUR HEAD

Dear God,

Thank You for the opportunity You have given me to play. Please help me execute with courage and to not be intimidated. Allow me to execute with confidence and conviction so that I can know the success of performing at a high level.

In Jesus' Name, Amen.

SPEED

When Urban Meyer became the Head Coach at the University of Florida, he stated that his goal was to have the fastest football team in America. During his tenure, Florida went to the Spread Option Offense and many thought it would never work in the SEC given the speed of the defenses. However, Meyer proved them all wrong. During his tenure he won two National Championships. The speed of Percy Harvin, Jeff Demps, Chris Rainey and Tim Tebow dominated their opponents.

SPEED! In an interview not long ago Meyer said, "I see teams all the time that have speed and don't know how to use it." Look what the Bible has to say about the Lord's speed:

"For the Lord will carry out His sentence on earth with speed and finality." (Romans 9:28, NIV)

Look at three areas of your life where speed has a direct impact.

Speed Impacts Your Life

The Bible tells us in James 4:14, *"What is your life? You are a mist that appears for a little while and then vanishes."* I can tell you that verse is so true. It doesn't seem like it was that long ago that I was in high school. I can remember it like it was yesterday, but it's been over 30 years ago. The older you get the faster life passes you by.

Do you realize that not many people get the opportunity to play in a game like this? So here's the question: Are you going to just plod through this thing and be a spectator; or are you going to make the most of this? I've learned from experience if you don't give your best you will look back on this day and wish you had.

Speed Impacts Your Play

Think about it. At every transition the game gets faster, doesn't it? When you moved up from Pop-Warner to Middle School, the game got faster. From Middle School to Junior Varsity it got a little faster. Then from Junior Varsity to Varsity things happen even faster. If you move from Varsity to College things will happen a lot faster. Then if you are fortunate enough to move from College to the NFL, *everybody* has speed and things happen like a flash of lightning.

> *"If what you did yesterday seems big, you haven't done anything today."*
>
> Lou Holtz

During the game you are going to see some speed. They have speed and you've got speed. You've prepared, you've practiced, and you have a game plan. They are not any better than you. If you will play fast, play physical, and play smart you'll be fine. I like what Lou Holtz says, "If what you did yesterday seems big, you haven't done anything today."

Speed Impacts Your Decisions

The decisions you make can cause things to happen

fast; both good and bad. A great example of this is what happened to one of your former teammates. It wasn't that long ago he was on the field playing just like you. He was a gifted athlete with limitless potential. Yet one night, because of a poor decision, he lost his life. The driver had been drinking and little did they know it would be the last night of your teammate's life. He wasn't planning on dying that night. In fact, I will guarantee you the thought never crossed his mind. But because of one mistake, it cost him and his family dearly.

How long does it take to make a decision? A minute? A second? A nanosecond? Just like that you can make a decision that will shape the rest of your life or end your life. In a split second you can be here in this world and then gone. In a matter of seconds you can make a decision that will haunt you and change the course of your life for years to come. Remember that the decisions you make can make things happen quickly. Making good decisions is crucial at every level.

Speed impacts every area of your life. It affects your physical life, your athletic life, and your spiritual life. How you handle speed will affect your life now, in the future, and for eternity.

BOW YOUR HEAD

Dear God,

I come asking that You grant me wisdom and strength. I pray that I will be reminded that this is an opportunity that few people have. I ask You to help me to use the physical speed I have to give my very best effort.

In Jesus' Name, Amen.

HEART

Have you ever thought about what separates winners from losers on the playing field? I believe you can boil it all down to one word, *heart*.

The Bible has something to say about the issue of heart.

"As in water face reflects face, so the heart of man reflects man." (Proverbs 27:19, NASB)

The Bible says that what's on the inside has a way of working itself to the outside. Just as you walk up to a pool of water and see your reflection, your heart will reveal the real you.

The name Sammy McCorkle probably doesn't mean anything to you. Sammy played for the University of Florida from 1992-1996. He was a three-time letterman. However, McCorkle made his mark on special teams. He was especially effective on kickoffs. When the ball was in the air, Sammy was like a missile heading for its target, the ball carrier. At 5'9" and 182 pounds he was a one-man wrecking crew. He was usually the first guy to the ball carrier to make the tackle. He had heart. If McCorkle had been 6'3" and 285 pounds you would have seen him play on Sundays in the NFL.

Joe Namath said, "If you aren't going all the way, why go at all?"

HEART. Here are four characteristics of people who play with heart:

People with Heart Show up Everyday

There is something inside that compels them to leave it all on the field. They realize that every day is an opportunity to get better. They don't take plays off, and they sure don't take days off. These are the people you can depend upon. These are the people upon whom you can build a program.

A characteristic of people with heart is that they are in the moment. They are totally engaged and totally committed to getting the job done. They give their very best effort every day.

> *"If you aren't going all the way, why go at all?"*
>
> *Joe Namath*

People with Heart Keep Improving

Did you know that there is a difference between knowing "how" to do something and "why" you do something? The person who knows "how" will always have a job, but the person who knows "why" will be the boss. People who are driven to be the best and give their whole heart to it have a tendency to always evaluate where they are and how they can get better.

Read this verse again:

"As in water face reflects face, so the heart of man reflects man." Take a step back and look at yourself. Is your heart in your practice and your play? Are you driven to get better? Or are you content with things the way they are?

People with Heart Follow Through
With Excellence

Jesus followed through. Aren't you glad He followed through? He could have said, "I'm not going to do everything. I'm not going to the cross. I'm not willing to make the sacrifice." I don't know about you, but I'm thankful that He finished what He came to do. I'm glad He followed through with excellence.

The next time you take the field your heart is going to be exposed. When the whistle blows and play begins the true story is going to be told. The crowd, the coaches, and the other team will walk away tonight saying one of two things. First, "That team has heart. They never quit and they finished strong." Or second they will say, "That team has a lot of talent and lots of potential, but they don't have heart."

People with Heart Inspire Others

People with heart have a way of lifting those around them to be better. Their play inspires others to play harder. Their effort creates momentum that can carry a team to victory.

I love the movie "Rudy." Talk about someone with heart, he had it. A walk-on at Notre Dame, he busted his backside every day on the scout team. He was beat up, knocked around, and yet he refused to quit, back down, or coast. He came to practice every day and gave everything he had. He inspired his team to the point that many of them were willing to sacrifice their ability to dress out just so he could dress out for one game. Then, instead of allowing the clock to run out, they scored again, even though the game was in hand, just to let him get in the game.

When you look in the mirror what do you see? Do you see a person who has real heart? Just as surely as you look into a pool of water and see your reflection, others will look at your life and performance and tell if you have heart.

BOW YOUR HEAD

Dear God,

As I play the next game, I pray that You will help me to reveal my heart. I pray that I give my very best and that my effort inspires others.

In Jesus' Name, Amen.

FAMILY

On July 25, 2010, Bob Hertzel wrote the following column for the *The Times West Virginia*:

"As the beginning of West Virginia's football camp draws closer and closer, now just a couple of weeks away, the time has come to begin thinking about just what this football thing is all about.

That is a deeper subject than you may give it credit for being, for those who believe football is just a game also believe that Ben & Jerry's is just an ice cream and Jimmy John's is just a sandwich shop.

Football is many things, and a game is almost the least

important part of it. Without getting into it too deeply, it is a test of man against man and a test of man against himself, a gut check and, at the same time, an intelligence test.

It is not life itself, but it well may be the closest thing we have come up with to imitate it.

See the season is its own universe, the game the challenges that life itself presents and the team ... ah, the team, that is the family unit, with coaches in the parental roles and teammates making up the brotherhood to which the players belong."

"Football is a game that you can't play alone and that you can't win if there is no glue to bond the brotherhood.

'It's knowing you don't have to do it all by yourself. You always have 10 other guys out there with you. You don't have to worry about doing it yourself,' senior nose guard Christ Neild said. 'When you feel that way, when you know you have guys behind you, you don't have that much to worry about.'

When things are going well, this isn't as important as it may seem. It's when things are at their lowest that you need each other the most.

This can be evidenced over the past few years, how this brotherhood concept builds strength in the entire unit."

FAMILY.   In the Old Testament book of Daniel there is a story that gives us a glimpse of what being a brotherhood, a family, is all about.

Shadrach, Meshach, and Abed-nego were servants of King Nebuchadnezzar of Babylon. Nebuchadnezzar was a very prideful king. He had a statue of himself built and put on display for everyone to see. He sent out a decree that whenever the people heard the royal orchestra play, they were to turn and bow down to the statue.

Shadrach, Meshach, and Abed-nego worshipped the one true God, so when the orchestra began to play they refused to bow with everyone else in the kingdom. Nebuchadnezzar was told of their unwillingness to bow and gave the three servants an opportunity to obey his command. Their response made Nebuchadnezzar furious. They said, "We won't even consider it. Our God will deliver us from any punishment you have for us."

Because they refused to bow to the golden statue, King Nebuchadnezzar ordered the furnace to be heated seven times hotter than it had ever been heated. He ordered Shadrach, Meshach, and Abed-nego to be thrown into the fire. The heat was so intense that those who threw them into the fire were devoured by the flames.

Finally, Nebuchadnezzar asked someone to look and see if the three had been totally devoured. One of the king's servants looked and said, "Didn't we throw three into the fire? I see four, and the fourth is like unto the Son of God!"

There are three simple truths about family that we learn from this story.

A Family Knows Who They Are

"There are certain Jews whom you have appointed over the administration of the province of Babylon, namely Shadrach, Meshach and Abed-nego. These men, O king, have disregarded you; they do not serve your gods or worship the golden image which you have set up." (Daniel 3:12, NASB)

These guys knew who they were. They refused to cave in and bend under pressure, and as a result, their character was put on full display for everyone to see. They understood what was at stake and they knew their identity. They were family.

Nobody knows family like family. On the outside you can look at a family, but you really don't know them. I know my family. I know every member of my family. I know what they need. I know what they like. I know what makes them tick. I know what makes them happy. I know what makes them mad. I'm all in where my family is concerned. If my family needs me, I'm there. When it comes to them I'm all in physically, emotionally, spiritually, financially—in every way.

Your team has spent enough time together that you know each other really well. Some of you have been together for four years or more. You've worked hard. You're a brotherhood, a family. A family encourages one another. A family cheers for one another. A family holds one another accountable. You are a Team! Here's the question: Are you all in for the family?

A Family Stays Together

"Shadrach, Meshach and Abed-nego replied to the king, 'O Nebuchadnezzar, we do not need to give you an answer concerning this matter.'" (Daniel 3:16, NASB)

Shadrach, Meshach, and Abed-Nego dared to stand up when everyone else was bowing down. They stood together and went against the flow of their culture. They didn't care what everyone else was saying. They didn't care what everyone else was doing. They stood together and placed their faith in God.

The next time your team is together take a look at "your family." Take a look at your brothers. Some of you are black and some of you are white. Some of you are fast and some of you are not as fast. Some of you are larger than others. Some of you are freshman and others seniors. But tonight when you put on that uniform and take the field you are a family.

> *"It's when things are at their lowest that you need each other the most."*
>
> Bob Hertzel

People are going to say what they are going to say. There will always be those who will second guess and complain. In their minds they are the experts. But it doesn't matter what anyone else says or does. All that matters is that you stay together because you are a family.

A family doesn't quit on one another. A family gives their best for one another. A family is all in for one another. When things get tough on the field, you are going to stand together because you are a family.

A Family Withstands the Fire

"If it be so, our God whom we serve is able to deliver us from the furnace of blazing fire; and He will deliver us out of your

hand, O king." (Daniel 3:17, NASB)

When the heat was on, they stood together. The furnace was heated seven times hotter than it had ever been. The fire was so hot the guards who threw them in were burned alive. Here's the point: When these guys were thrown into the fire they never flinched, they didn't back down, they didn't back out, they stood together!

Standing together isn't as important when everything is going right. However, it gets critical when things don't go your way. When the call doesn't go your way, stand together. When the momentum switches to the other side, stand together. If you will stay together you can withstand the fire.

"He said, 'Look! I see four men loosed and walking about in the midst of the fire without harm, and the appearance of the fourth is like a son of the gods!'" (Daniel 3:25, NASB)

Here are seven things that will help you withstand adversity:

1. Trust God regardless of the circumstances.

2. Always remember that no matter how bad things are, they are going to get better.

3. Never, ever, ever give up!

4. You only have one life, so make the best of the life God has given you.

5. God uses adversity to make you better.

6. Be persistent and resilient, and when you are tired and you feel you cannot go another step, press on.

7. Life is not a destination, it is a journey so enjoy the ride.

BOW YOUR HEAD

Dear God,

I thank You for my brothers and for the opportunity we have to stand together. I pray that You will bind us together and that You receive glory from our lives.

In Jesus' Name, Amen.

CHARACTER

J ohn Wooden, former legendary basketball coach who won 10 NCAA titles at UCLA, said, "Sports do not build character, they reveal it."

Think of it this way. If I take a bottle of mustard and hold it up, how do I know what's in it? From all appearances it looks like a bottle of mustard. The label on the bottle says, "mustard." I can shake it and I can hear something in the bottle. I can smell it and it can smell like mustard. However, the only way I can truly find out if it is mustard is to squeeze the bottle and see what comes out.

That's the way character works. Whenever you are squeezed, what is on the inside comes out. You see, when you take the field, from all appearances you are going to look like a football team. Your uniforms say that you are a football team. You're going to sound like a football team when you warm up. You'll even smell like a football team when you're in the locker room. However, the true test will come when you get squeezed. Your character is going to be revealed tonight like it or not, win or lose. Football will not build your character, but it will definitely reveal it.

The apostle Paul has something to say about character in Romans 5:4. Read what he had to say.

> "Sports do not build character, they reveal it."
>
> John Wooden

"*And not only this, but we also exult in our tribulations, knowing that tribulation brings about perseverance; and perseverance, proven character; and proven character, hope.*" (Romans 5:3-4, NASB)

CHARACTER. What does it look like? How can you evaluate the level of your character? There are four things that will help you measure your character. How you live and the character you display will be something that you will need to measure throughout your life.

People of Character Are Trustworthy

A trustworthy person is an honest person. They don't lie, cheat, or steal. They follow through. They are reliable, dependable, and loyal. They have the courage to do what is right. They will stand by their family, their friends, and their team.

In this context, "Are you trustworthy?" You have a game to play. Can your team depend on you? When you step out onto that field, your coaches and your teammates are placing their trust in you. You have a job to perform, and the team is depending on you to do what you have said you would do. You are in essence saying, "I'm going to do my job the way I've been coached for the benefit of my team."That's what it means to stand by your team.

People of Character Show Respect

This is simple. All you have to do is follow the golden rule, *"do unto others as you would have them do unto you."* Be a good sport. Use good manners. Be considerate of others. Show respect.

This is not to say that you are supposed to be soft. You play all out! Give everything you have on every play. When the play is over, help the guy up and go back to the huddle. Don't get caught up in anything that would show disrespect to your team. Your coach always tells you not to retaliate because usually the second guy is the one who gets the flag and costs the team. Show respect to the coaches, the officials, the other team and your team. In other words show your character and have a little class.

People of Character Take Responsibility

Taking responsibility is doing what you are supposed to do. It means carrying out your responsibilities. It means taking responsibility for your actions and your attitude, and using self-control. It means growing up and admitting it's not all about you, but the team.

What are you responsible for in the next game you play? Whatever it may be, you need to own it! Do it to the best of your ability. Accepting responsibility is a part of life. Mature people accept responsibility. If you don't take care of your responsibilities on the field it can cost you the game. However, if you don't take care of your responsibilities in life, it can cost you your job, your family, your marriage, or negatively impact your future. How you handle your responsibilities says a lot about your character.

In other words, play by the rules. Don't blame others for your mistakes. If you make a mistake, put it behind you and move on. You can't undo what's been done. Get ready for the next play and be accountable.

One thing is certain, you are going to be squeezed during the game. It's going to be a battle. They are going to make some plays and you are going to make some plays. Show strong character in the midst of the battle. Be trustworthy, show respect, take responsibility, and be fair. Abraham Lincoln said, "Nearly all men can stand adversity, but if you want to test a man's character, give him success."

BOW YOUR HEAD

Dear God,

Thank You for opportunities to be tested. Sometimes You allow us to be squeezed to let us see what's on the inside. You already know what's there. I pray that when the test comes and I am squeezed in the heat of battle, my true character will be revealed.

In Jesus' Name, Amen.

EFFORT

Tim Tebow may be one of the best college football players in recent history. In January 2009, Florida faced off against Oklahoma in the BCS Championship game played in Miami, Florida. At the end of the second quarter the score was tied 7-7. As the players entered the locker room during halftime, Tim Tebow stood in the center of the room and challenged his teammates by yelling, "Thirty minutes for the rest of our lives! Thirty minutes for the rest of our lives!"

In his speech, Tim was challenging his teammates to give it all they had for the next 30 minutes of game play. By the end of the third quarter the score was Florida 14 – Oklahoma 7. The Gators continued to give it all they had during the fourth quarter, winning over Oklahoma 24- 14.

EFFORT. If you want to be the best, you've got to get out on the field and give it all you've got. You've got to give the effort that is needed. Lou Holtz says, "It's not the load that breaks you down, it's the way you carry it."

The writer of Ecclesiastes is perhaps the wisest man to ever live. His name was Solomon.

Read what Solomon had to say about effort:

"Whatever your hand finds to do, do it with all your might." (Ecclesiastes 9:10, NASB)

In other words, whatever you do, you should give your very best effort.

There are four things that can help you as you evaluate the effort that you are giving to your team:

Desire

Ask yourself: "Do I really want to do this?" Because if you don't, you're not going to give your best effort. You know it's easy to give lip service to wanting to win a game or live a life that honors God, but deep down in your gut you know whether you want to or not. If you do, then you will give the maximum effort. If you don't, you won't give your best.

You may say, "Well, I want to live a life that honors God." If that's true, then turn the X-Box off, pick up a Bible and see what God has to say to you. You say, "I want to go the playoffs." Then execute the way you need to execute. You've worked hard to get to this point. You've sacrificed and paid the price. All of that will be in vain if you don't want it bad enough to do what has to be done.

Accountability

People of effort are accountable. They are not afraid to be held accountable. They don't hide behind excuses. They accept responsibility for their assignments and own up to mistakes when they make them. They realize that accountability makes them better and keeps them motivated.

If you aren't what you ought to be, why not exert a little effort and fix it? If your attitude is bad, change it. If you continue to make careless mistakes, stop it. If you've not been giving your maximum effort, then start. Football and life are not about you alone. You have a team to whom you are accountable. One day you will have a family, a boss, colleagues, and others who will hold you accountable. Ultimately you are accountable to God. He is the ultimate accountability partner. Remember that what you do will have a direct impact on more people than just you. Be accountable!

Consistency

To be consistent you need to be intentional. Do you know what you need to do to develop bad habits? Nothing. Bad habits develop naturally. Everything in life that is worth having takes effort.

Following Christ takes effort. The Bible says we must be consistent and renew our minds every day. If we don't make an effort to do it, it won't happen. Your faith is not just a one day a week thing. Your faith is a relationship with Almighty God. Every day He wants to lead and guide you. He wants to talk to you. He wants you to talk to Him. He is interested in what you are doing and what you dream of doing. He wants to use you for His glory and your good.

Repetition

Why do you practice so hard every week? So you

can get reps, right? You keep doing the same thing right over and over until you play without thinking— you play fast. You've done the same thing over and over so much that it has become second nature to you. That takes effort.

Walter Payton was one of the greatest players in NFL history. He said, "I want to be remembered as the guy who gave his all whenever he was on the field." If you've ever watched a highlight film on him, you know he believed what he said.

> ***"I want to be remembered as the guy who gave his all whenever he was on the field."***
>
> *Walter Payton*

He gave the maximum effort possible.

How about you? How bad do you want it? Are you willing to step up and give the effort? Have you been intentional about being the best you can be? And have you committed to putting in the reps necessary to get the job done? It takes effort to succeed.

BOW YOUR HEAD

Dear God,

I thank You for everything that has been accomplished for me and my team. As we play this season, help us, as players and coaches, to give the effort that is needed to reach our goals.

In Jesus' Name, Amen.

WIN

V incent Lombardi is arguably the greatest football coach of all time, and is on the short list of greatest coaches ever. His ability to teach, motivate and inspire players helped turn the Green Bay Packers into the most dominating NFL team in the 1960's.

Lombardi became a hot commodity in the coaching arena. He accepted the head coaching position and signed a five-year contract with the Green Bay Packers in January 1959. From the very beginning he established himself as a coach firmly in charge. He conducted grueling training camps and demanded absolute dedication and effort from his players. His hard-nosed style turned the Packers into the most successful franchise in the 1960's, leading them to five NFL Championships, including victories in Super Bowls I and II, and solidifying Lombardi's status as the greatest football coach in history.

Vince Lombardi knew something about winning. He said, "If it doesn't matter who wins or loses, then why do they keep score?" Make no mistake about it; we are playing games to win.

WIN. The writer of Hebrews gives us some insight in how to win.

"...*let us also lay aside every encumbrance and the sin which so easily entangles us, and let us run with endurance the race that is set before us*..." (Hebrews 12:1, NASB)

The race is set before you. What does it mean to win? Let's take the word "*win*" and use it in an acrostic to help us understand what it means.

W—Work Hard!

That's simple enough isn't it? Whatever you do, work hard and do your best. If you're a coach, do your best coaching. If you're a starter, do your best on the field. If you're on the sidelines, do your best encouraging your teammates. If you're a water boy, do the best job you can getting the water to the team when they need it. When you give your best effort it means that you give your all. Once you give everything you have and do the best job you can, no one can ask for anything else.

This is a great discipline to develop in life. The Bible says, *"Whatever you do in word or deed, do all in the name of the Lord Jesus..."* (Col. 3:17) Winners want to be the best at what they do. If you are a football player, be the best football player you can be. If you are a teacher, doctor, lawyer, plumber, electrician...be the best you can be. Work hard and do your very best.

I—Invest Your Time and Talents

You've worked hard and put in the time. If you train hard it will not only make you hard, but it will make you hard to beat. But in order to do this you've got to buy in to what you're trying to accomplish.

So what do you get when you invest, buy in and work hard? This builds character, it transforms you, increases your confidence, makes you better, gets you ahead, causes you to grow, and gives you an opportunity to fight the saboteur who said you couldn't do it. You get the idea. Really nothing worthwhile comes easily.

People who win are invested. What kind of investment are you making in life? Believe it or not, what you are doing today will impact your future. Your education is of great importance. Without a good education, you are going to have a hard time. You've got to invest in your future. Get your education! Go be the best you can be for the glory of God.

N—Never Quit!

In other words, winners are persistent. When I think about persistence I think of a baby trying to walk. They fail hundreds of times yet they never give up. Eventually they learn to take a few wobbly steps and fall down again. They get back up and one day they are running around the yard. Think about it. They never give in, never give up, and never give over to the challenge. They just keep getting up and trying again.

> *Persistence means taking little baby steps, never giving up, finding ways to overcome obstacles.*

Persistence means taking little baby steps, never giving up, finding ways to overcome obstacles. Where would we be if the Wright Brothers had given up, if Ben Franklin had decided not to fly a kite? Walt Disney went bankrupt before he finally broke through with Disney Land. Colonel Sanders received over a thousand no's before someone was finally willing to take a chance on him. Look where Kentucky Fried Chicken is today. So if you ever think about quitting, go find the nearest baby and watch them.

Winning has a lot to do with attitude. Remember the scripture? The Bible says, *"lay aside every encumbrance…and run with endurance the race that is set before us."* There will be things that weigh you down and hinder your progress. Some of you need to lay aside bad attitudes, bad influencers, hurtful words, destructive actions, and a number of other things that would keep you from being the best, being a winner. Lay it aside and make up your mind that you are going to run this race with endurance and win.

Notice the runner of this race does not have a thought of failure. His only focus is finishing the race well. You know what's ahead. So take the challenge, finish well and win!

BOW YOUR HEAD

Dear God,

I thank You that my team is full of winners. We are tenacious and determined. I pray that we would give our best because we have invested much. Adjust our thinking and give us the strength that we will need to run the race that is before us.

In Jesus' Name, Amen.

ENDURANCE

D oes anyone remember which game was the longest game in college football history? It was the November 1, 2003, game between the Arkansas Razorbacks and the Kentucky Wildcats. After almost 5 hours, the game was finally won in the seventh overtime by Arkansas with a score of 71-63.

After the game Houston Nutt, the coach for Arkansas, said, "As long as we get to seven (overtimes), it's OK. The game was meant for us and we believe we're going to win in overtime." The team was prepared for overtime. Two years prior Arkansas beat Mississippi 58-56 in seven overtimes. The Razorbacks knew how to endure to the end.

As an athlete that's what you prepare for. You have been disciplined in your training, enduring strenuous practice routines, because you have been focused on the goal of succeeding.

The Bible tells us that God does allow life to get difficult at times so that we can be made holy. Even though God's discipline is painful, it produces righteousness and peace. Just as elite athletes push themselves to endure pain during a race by focusing on pre-planned thoughts and goals, we are to rely on Jesus for encouragement and strength when we are running our life race.

"Brethren, I do not regard myself as having laid hold of it yet; but one thing I do, forgetting what lies behind and reaching forward to what lies ahead, I press on toward the goal for the prize of the upward call of God in Christ Jesus." (Philippians 3:13-14, NASB)

ENDURANCE. There are three things that will help you run with endurance the race of life and play with endurance today:

Remember it's a Marathon, Not a Sprint

The apostle Paul said, *"I do not regard myself as having laid hold of it yet..."* In other words, I'm not there yet. I haven't finished the race. I'm in process.

As athletes this should speak to you. You are familiar with the process because you are in it. You understand that there is always work to do. There is preparation to be made. Each game brings its own challenges. The season is going to be long and there will be high points and low points. The goal is to get better each week and peak at the right time.

Life is not that much different. Life is a process and there is always work to be done and challenges to face. The goal in life is to keep your focus on the right things and run the race well.

Here are some keys to running the race well. You can apply these things on the field and in life.

- **Enjoy the journey.** Believe it or not, these are the best days of your life so enjoy them. These are your "good ole days." This period of your life will never come again. Each game you play will be one less. So make the most of this opportunity. Enjoy the journey.

- **Stay on schedule.** In every game you need to stay on schedule. You have goals about how many yards you want to face on the third down and how many yards you allow the opponent to gain rushing. Penalties and poor execution get you off schedule and can cause you problems that can cost you the game. In life you need to stay on schedule too. Poor decisions and mistakes can get you off schedule and cost you in many ways. It's imperative that you run your race of life on schedule; God's schedule.

- **Focus on the goal.** In sports the goal is to win the game, win the conference, the region, the state. However, there is a bigger goal than that. The goal is to be like Christ in every way. When you are on the field you should reflect Christ in your actions and attitudes. In life the goal is to hear Jesus say, "Well done! You ran a great race! I'm so proud of your effort and the way you endured the journey."

Life is a marathon, not a sprint. That's why you enjoy the journey, stay on schedule, and focus on the goal.

You've Got to Take Out the Trash

Scripture also says, *"Forgetting what lies behind and reaching forward to what lies ahead..."* In life and in sports it's not always the big things that bring the greatest consequences; sometimes it's the little things. It's the details that you overlook. The amazing thing is that small things, that seem insignificant at the time, have a way of piling up until they end up tripping you up.

It's just like running a race wearing a heavy backpack. Let's say in the beginning there is nothing in the pack. Then there are small things, insignificant things, that we don't deal with and they get added to the pack. Those things start adding up and eventually it is going to slow you down. Sin gets in the way of your ability to live your life in a way that honors God. Sin consumes our time and energy and takes our focus off God, slowing us down in our life race.

So how do you guard against this? The Bible says in Romans 12:2, "*And do not be conformed to this world, but be transformed* **by the renewing of your mind**, *so that you may prove what the will of God is, that which is good and acceptable and perfect.*" You've got to renew your mind. Renewing your mind is like taking out the trash. If you don't empty the trash it begins to smell and everyone knows there is something rotten in the house.

Here are two steps to renewing your mind:

- **Your failures must be relinquished.** That means don't keep making the same mistake over and over again. And don't keep kicking yourself for the mistake you made. Learn from it, let it go, and move on! This builds character.

- **Your victories must be remembered.** Remember the victories. Remember when you got it right and did it right. If you did it once you can do it again. This builds confidence.

Taking out the trash is deliberate. It doesn't happen all by itself. It is something that you've got to do. So when you make a mistake (and you will) learn from it and move on. When you win a major victory enjoy it, celebrate it, and get ready for the next challenge.

You Determine to Finish Well

"*...and let us run with endurance the race that is set before us...*" Since life is a marathon not a sprint, it's not so much how you start but how you finish.

I've got a rule at my house: "What you start, you finish." I haven't made any of my kids sign up for something they didn't want to do. If they chose to play a sport or join an organization, it's because they really wanted to do it. But they know that if they start it, they will finish it. When you finish well—when you run with endurance, you put your character on display for everyone to see.

Here are three things to remember about finishing well:

- **You are not running alone**. We don't do it alone in life or in sports. In life you have family and friends who are running with you. Somehow it makes it easier when we realize that we are not alone.

- **Life is a tough race.** Life is not fair. Life will challenge you. It's full of ups and downs. There will be good days and bad days. You take it as it comes and you keep running; you endure.

- **Everyone's race is different.** God's plan for each of us is different. The challenges will not be the same. You've got to decide how you are going to run your race. Run your race without regret.

When all is said and done, do you have the desire to finish well? Do you want to finish the game well? Do you want to finish your life well? Remember life is a journey; cherish it. Victories are to be remembered. God has created you to run this race, and He has equipped you and is empowering you to finish the race well.

BOW YOUR HEAD

Dear God,

I thank You for the life You have given me. You have given me a race to run and a life to live. I pray that my life will glorify You and that I will finish well.

In Jesus' Name, Amen.

FIGHT

Les Miles, Head Football Coach of the LSU Tigers, is building a dynasty in Louisiana. I believe that the key to his success is that he has been successful in building a sense of team. If you've watched LSU you know that "the mad hatter" is not afraid to roll the dice and gamble at the most unexpected time. His players and coaches love him; they want to play and work for him. LSU is physical and will fight you until the last second ticks off of the game clock.

Miles is also a strong family man. He has built his home on the right foundation and his wife and children believe he is absolutely awesome! He is never too busy for his family. It's not uncommon to see his children running through the athletic offices or watching practices. In spite of his busy schedule, he makes it a point to be home for dinner each night with his family when he's in town.

I believe that Les Miles understands that in order to build a successful team you have to be willing to fight. You have to fight to be the best. You have to fight for your family in the midst of an incredibly busy life.

Did you know that the Bible has something to say about fighting the good fight?

"I have fought the good fight, I have finished the course, I have kept the faith." (2 Timothy 4:7, NASB)

Look at your fist for a moment. When I hold up my fists to you it says, "Let's fight." Your fist is made up of five fingers. Four of them deliver the impact. Each finger is important and has a purpose. When you hold your fist up to your teammates and coaches it should be a silent reminder of your commitment.

FIGHT. Here are four things that will help you to remember what it takes to fight together as a team. In fact, these four things can be building blocks that you can use for the rest of your life:

F—Family

The first finger in the fist is family. In any successful team there is always a sense of family or togetherness. Families love each other, encourage each other, and hold each other accountable. You have busted your backsides to get where you are today. The guys on your team are your brothers. You have worked, sweated, sacrificed, and labored together to get to this point. You've built a bond that will last. You have experienced the thrill of victory and the agony of defeat. You have grown close and for the rest of your life, you'll never forget this family.

I—Integrity

The second finger in the fist is integrity. Integrity says I'll do my part. I'll give my best. I'm buying in completely for the good of the team. I'll take my responsibility seriously. I'm willing to be held accountable. When I get in the fight, I will be committed to do my job to the best of my ability. Both coaches and players must make this commitment.

You can't be a person of integrity and not fulfill your responsibility. You can't loaf, take plays off, or give less than your best effort. Integrity says I'm going to do what I've agreed to do. Like it or not, when you take the field you accept responsibility for your job.

S—Sincerity

The third finger in the fist is sincerity. Sincerity says I'm invested and on board. You've set some goals. You've already achieved some of them, but not all of them. If you're going to achieve all of your goals as a team, you've got to be sincere, you've got to care.

Winning teams care about things. They give attention to details. They focus on what is in front of them. They understand that the

> **"Trust is the most important part of a team."**

secret to success is in the details, and they make sure they are in the right position. They pay attention and concentrate on their assignment. They follow through and don't quit.

T—Trust

The fourth finger in the fist is trust. Trust is the most important part of a team. When you trust each other you begin to develop a culture where you believe you're going to win. You look into your teammates eyes and they look into your eyes and you believe in them and they believe in you. You have established a culture of trust. Competing becomes fun and winning becomes intoxicating.

Look at your fist again. Five fingers, four that make an impact, curled up and pressed together to pack a punch. Their force and power hinges on the fact that they support each other.

Suppose you were to make a fist and curl up all but one finger. What kind of a punch would you pack? Not much of one, right? How about all but two fingers? You have virtually no power in your punch. But when you put them together: family, integrity, sincerity, and trust, you are ready to fight the good fight and win because of the power of unity.

BOW YOUR HEAD

Dear God,

I come to You today and ask You to bring my team together and harness our energy, strength, and ability to fight the good fight.

In Jesus' Name, Amen.

INTENSITY

Mike Singletary, linebacker for the Chicago Bears, was one intense player. He finished as the Bears' first or second leading tackler each of his last 11 seasons. He amassed an impressive 1,488 career tackles, 885 of which were solo efforts. A constant force on defense, he missed playing in just two games, both in 1986.

His best performance as a pro was when he recorded 10 solo tackles and 10 assists in 1990 in a game against the Denver Broncos. He was selected to play in a team record 10 Pro Bowls; he was All-Pro eight times and All-NFC every year from 1983 until 1991.

When you watched him play he was all business. He

would knock your head off. Famous for the wild look in his eyes just before the snap of the ball, he was a picture of intensity.

Coach Pat Street said, "Intensity must last to the last whistle." People of intensity are focused, driven, passionate, and determined.

The Old Testament gives us a snapshot of a person of intensity. His name was Samson. He was the "Heavy Weight Champion" of the Bible. As the strongest man to ever live, his story is fascinating and he is a case study of a person who is intense.

In one verse he tells his story:

"With the jawbone of a donkey I have killed a thousand men." (Judges 15:16, NASB)

I'd say that's pretty intense!

INTENSITY. There are three things that we can learn from the life of Samson about intensity:

People of Intensity Are Confident In Their Ability

Samson knew he was strong. He knew his strength

was a gift from God and that the secret to his strength was his hair. Samson had taken the vow of a Nazarite—meaning that he could not cut his hair, could not touch a dead

> **"Intensity must last to the last whistle."**
>
> *Pat Street*

body, and could not drink any strong drink. As long as he didn't cut his hair his strength would not leave. However, if he cut his hair his strength would be gone.

Think about your teammates for a moment. There are all kinds of talents and abilities represented on your team. Don't ever forget who you are and where your gifts came from. Any ability you have is God given. You may develop a gift, but God made you the way you are. Samson knew that there wasn't a man walking the planet who could whip him, but he also knew that it was God who had given him his ability.

People of Intensity Dig Deep

You think Samson didn't dig deep? The Philistines hated him. They couldn't wait to see Samson fall. They wanted him dead. Samson stood in front of the Philistine army with the jawbone of a donkey in his hand and took on all of them. When the battle was over 1,000 Philistine soldiers lay dead on the battlefield and Samson was the last man standing.

People of intensity do not run from a challenge, they run to the challenge. They don't retreat, they relish the opportunity to compete.

Steve Spurrier is a picture of intensity. Famous for throwing his visor in frustration on the sidelines, he is an intense and passionate coach. His father was a Presbyterian Pastor, and several years ago I had the opportunity to meet him. As the conversation turned toward his son Mr. Spurrier said, "Steve is probably the most intense and competitive person I know. If he is playing you in a game of Tiddlywinks he is going to try to beat you." People of intensity are "in it to win it." Samson never had a thought of defeat. He just took care of business when the challenge presented itself.

People of Intensity Forget About Their Mistakes and Step Up When Needed

Samson met and fell in love with a woman named Delilah. The Philistines convinced Delilah to find out the secret to Samson's strength. So Delilah came to Samson and began to question him about the secret of his strength. After lying to her three times about the source of his strength, he finally confessed that his strength was tied to his hair. While he slept, Delilah called a man in to shave his head. When Samson awoke, he realized he had lost his strength and was captured by the Philistines.

Once the Philistines had him in captivity they gouged out his eyes and put him in prison. Later they brought him to their temple and tied him between two pillars. As they made fun of him he cried out to God, "God, restore my strength just one more time and let me die here with these Philistines." God granted his wish and Samson, in a final act of strength, pulled down the pillars of the temple on top of them all. He killed more in this last act of strength than he had killed during his entire life.

People of intensity forget about their mistakes and step up when needed. In life you will make mistakes. During your next game you will probably make some mistakes. When you make them, learn what you can, forget about them, and move on. If you drive down the road and stare in the rearview mirror instead of looking through the windshield, you are going to have a wreck. Glance at the past, but focus on the future. Focus on the next play in the game or the next chapter of your life. You can't do anything about the past, but you can do something about the opportunity before you.

BELIEVE

Which NFL team started the season as a 50-1 long shot to win it all? It was the 2001 New England Patriots. Kurt Warner and the St. Louis Rams, on the other hand, seemed on their way to building a football dynasty by dominating their opponents with an explosive offense. The Rams finished off the 2001 season with a 14-2 record. The Patriots, however, barely made the playoffs with a record of 11-5.

The Patriots, led by Quarterback Tom Brady, arrived in New Orleans for Super Bowl XXXVI as 14-point underdogs, and came away 20-17 winners on Adam Vinatieri's 48-yard field goal on the last play of the game. It was one of the most exciting Super Bowls ever, and the greatest upset since the New York Jets beat the Baltimore Colts in Super Bowl III.

The Patriots won it all because they believed they could. At the beginning of the year nobody gave them a chance. But they believed and they fought their way to a championship.

In the Bible there is a story of a battle that was a long shot. The Philistines and Israel were at war and the Philistine army had marched out their champion, a literal giant named Goliath. The Philistines were issuing a winner-take-all challenge to anyone willing to stand up and fight against Goliath. If Goliath won, the Philistines would be victorious. However, if Israel's champion won, Israel would be declared the winner of the battle. The problem was that no one in Israel was willing to fight Goliath.

David had been sent by his father Jesse to the battle front to take supplies to his brothers who were soldiers in Israel's army. Upon his arrival, David heard Goliath issue the challenge and saw that there was no one willing to fight, so he stepped up and took the challenge.

- Here you have a boy that was willing to step up and fight like a man.

- On paper this was no fight. Goliath was bigger, stronger, and more experienced. He was a seasoned warrior.

- Nobody was giving David a fighting chance. But David believed and had confidence that he was going to win.

BELIEVE. Anytime you find a person or team faced with a challenge, there are four things that should always be present.

You Have Confidence You Will Win

David never considered defeat. It was not in his vocabulary. It was not on his mind. He never considered that he might lose. He was not afraid, and when he heard Goliath issue that challenge, he told the King that he would kill the uncircumcised Philistine.

When you believe—you don't hope or think you are going to win—you *know*. The confidence of victory is deeply seated in your mind and emotions to the point that you become fearless. You *will* yourself to win. Coach Paul "Bear" Bryant said, "There's no substitute for guts." People who have guts are confident.

When David stepped forward to take the challenge he was asked what qualified him to fight this battle. David said, "I have killed both a lion and a bear while watching my father's sheep, and this giant will be no different." David had learned from previous battles. They had prepared him for this moment.

> *"There's no substitute for guts."*
>
> *Paul "Bear" Bryant*

You have already started your journey. You've learned some valuable lessons in the process. All of that comes together, and because of where you've been and what you've experienced, you believe.

You Stand Courageously

As David walks out on the battlefield, all he is armed with is a slingshot and 5 smooth stones. He was prepared to take on all who showed up to fight. There was one stone for Goliath and a stone for each of Goliath's four brothers. Goliath, on the other hand, was armed to the max.

- He had a coat of mail. (armor)

- He had a javelin. (spear)
- He had a helmet.
- He had a shield.

On the outside he looked like a walking tank. He looked like he couldn't be beat. However, David never blinked. He stood courageously, loaded the sling with the first stone and let it fly. The stone hit Goliath in the one spot where he was vulnerable—right in the forehead, and he crumbled to the ground. David won the battle because he believed!

Every opponent is vulnerable. Every opponent has a weakness. So no matter how good your opponent, you must stand courageously, believe you're going to win, and hit them in their weak spot.

You Finish the Assignment Enthusiastically

When Goliath hit the ground, David took his sword and cut off his head. In other words, he didn't leave any doubt who the winner was. He finished his assignment enthusiastically.

"Then David ran and stood over the Philistine and took his sword and drew it out of its sheath and killed him, and cut off his head with it. When the Philistines saw that their champion was dead, they fled." (1 Samuel 17:51, NASB)

You have an opportunity to make a statement and send a message that your team is for real. You have a chance to leave no doubt as to who the better team is.

- They've come to your field of battle.

- They've got to contend with your fans.

- Let's cut the head off of this thing and leave no doubt as to who the better team is.

- Send them running for the buses after the battle is over.

Don't blink. Believe!

BOW YOUR HEAD

Dear God,

I thank you for your Word and that I can be encouraged by the story of David and Goliath. Give me the confidence and courage I need in the game and in life.

In Jesus name, Amen.

TEAM

Many consider the 1971 version of the Nebraska Cornhuskers the best college football team ever and I can't find any reason to disagree. This team averaged more than 39 points a game on offense, and surrendered only 8.2 points a game. Led by kick and punt returner Johnny Rodgers (who won the 1972 Heisman), the top-ranked Cornhuskers defeated No. 2 Oklahoma 35-31 on Thanksgiving Day, in what some have called the "Game of the Century." They rounded out their 13-0 season with a 38-6 thrashing of Alabama in the Orange Bowl.

The key to their success is that they were a team. There are many definitions for team. The one I like the best is "**T**ogether **E**veryone **A**ccomplishes **M**ore."

A team understands that as individuals they are limited, but together they are limitless. Team members understand that it is not about "me" but about "us." A team has chemistry, a spark, confidence, swagger, and the "it" factor.

In the Bible, long before football was even thought of, Jesus Christ was building a team that would have a tremendous impact on the whole world. These 12 men would turn the world upside down.

TEAM. What was it that enabled them to make such an impact? When you take a close look at this bunch there are three things that made them who they were as a team.

They Were Different

These twelve men came from all walks of life. Peter, James, John and Andrew were fishermen. Matthew was a tax-collector. Judas was a traitor and Simon was a religious fanatic. Thomas would be known as a doubter. Doesn't sound like a group that is going to change the world, does it? And it sure doesn't sound like a group that was going to transform the climate of humanity.

Believe it or not, diversity is a strength. Each one of

these guys brought something to the table that would make the group stronger and more effective.

Likewise, on your team you've got everything you need to succeed. This is not a one dimensional group. There is diversity on your team.

- You've got introverts and extroverts.
- You've got big and small.
- You've got fast and slow.
- You've got seasoned and rookies.

These differences work to your favor. Just because you are different doesn't mean you can't be a team. The very fact that you are different gives you the opportunity to be a great team.

They Were Devoted

These twelve men were completely devoted to Jesus Christ. They were willing to pay the price to get the job done. In fact, when Jesus called them to be a part of His team, He challenged them to leave the confines and comforts of their homes and follow Him. They were willing to do this because they believed in the cause.

Every effective team believes in the cause. The time,

the sacrifice, the effort, the work, the sweat, and the tears are endured because they believed in what they were doing.

I hope you believe in your team. I hope you believe in your cause. If you do, you are going to be just fine. If you don't, you're wasting your time. The twelve apostles were devoted to the cause, to Jesus, and to one another.

> *"Believe it or not, diversity is a strength."*

As long as you live you'll remember the guys on your team. There is a bond that has been built that will last for the rest of your lives. I remember the guys on my team: Kim Miller, Mike Crutchfield, Michael Clark, Jeffrey Cooper, Donnie Coker, Keith Newton, Darrell Olds, Steve Fowler, Greg Nolan, Gary Ward...I could go on and on. We were devoted to one another, and still are to some degree. A team pulls together, pays the price and does what they have to do to get the job done.

They Were Dynamic

After Jesus died, this team flourished and did some amazing things. Peter, the fisherman, blossomed into a great preacher. James and John became courageous missionaries. Andrew had a passion for his mission and did things that had never been done before. The book of Acts tells us that these men were accused of turning the whole world upside down.

A team is dynamic. They have the "it" factor. They know who they are as individuals, as well as who they are as a team. A dynamic team knows what they are here to do and what it takes to get the job done.

Remember this: "Team work makes the dream work." What's the dream? What's the goal? Where's the finish line? What is the "win" for this team? What is it, that after all is said and done, you can look at and say "we accomplished our goal?" You won't get there alone. It's going to take every member of your team working together, pulling together, and pressing together to get the job done.

BOW YOUR HEAD

Dear God,

Bring us together as individuals to build a great team. Build our love and devotion to each other. I pray that You will dynamically energize us and develop us into the best team we can be.

In Jesus' Name, Amen.

DISCIPLINE

If you watch SEC football then you are familiar with Courtney Upshaw, one-time linebacker for the University of Alabama. Upshaw is intense, persistent, ferocious, and extremely disciplined. In fact, in the 2011 Capital One Bowl, he led the way to a 49-7 victory for the Crimson Tide. During the game, Upshaw recorded a pair of sacks, five tackles, including three for a loss, as well as forcing a Michigan State fumble, and was voted the game's MVP.

In an interview on ESPN, Upshaw said that the one thing that Coach Saban had instilled in them as players was to be disciplined. When asked how the Crimson Tide was able to accumulate so few penalties he said, "You really don't want Coach Saban yelling at you.

We've all seen Coach Saban go off on people when they go out and do something stupid that can hurt us."

There is a phrase at the end of 1 Corinthians 9:24 that really speaks to this whole issue of discipline.

"Do you not know that those who run in a race all run, but only one receives the prize? Run in such a way that you may win." (1 Corinthians 9:24, NASB)

"Run in such a way that you may win." In other words, the way you run will dictate the results. The way you live your life will dictate the results. The way you apply yourself, the way you do your job, the way you treat your family, and the way you play the game today will all dictate the results!

Coach Bobby Knight, a living legend, says "Everyone wants to win, but not everyone is willing to prepare to win." Winning involves discipline.

DISCIPLINE. Here are three things that will help you measure your discipline:

Desire Is the Foundation of Discipline

You've got to get gut level honest with yourself and

ask this question, "Do I really want to?" That is the beginning point to anything. Do you really want to get an education? Do you really want to be a team? Do you really want to succeed in life? Do you really want to be the best? Do you really want to?

The way you answer that question will dictate the outcome. If you want to get an education, you apply yourself and do what you need to do. If you want to succeed in life, you determine what you need to do and get it done. If you want to be the best, you buy in, do what the coaches are asking of you, and give everything you have. It's called discipline, and the only kind of discipline that lasts is self-discipline. You've got to decide for you. No one else can make that decision for you.

Decisions Are the Conduit for Discipline

Once you determine that you really want it, you make the decision to get it done. In other words, flip the switch. Think about it: so much of what we do in this life involves flipping a switch. If I want to go somewhere I get in my car,

"Everyone wants to win, but not everyone is willing to prepare to win."

Bobby Knight

put the key in the ignition, and flip the switch. If I walk into a room that is dark and I want to see, I flip the switch. If I want to work on a paper, I get my laptop and turn it on, flip the switch and go to work. If I want to watch a ballgame, I pick up the remote, turn it on, flip the switch, and watch the game.

This is important. Everything about discipline involves a deep personal desire; but it can't stop there. You adjust your thinking by saying, "I'm going to do it!" You just can't talk about it. Talk is cheap. The world is full of big talkers. It's a matter of your will. Deep down inside of you, you have to flip that switch and decide to get the job done.

Determination Gives You the Drive for Discipline

Determination means not letting anything stand in your way. What is the thing that is standing in your way? Is it fear? Is it indifference? Is it a loss of confidence? What is the thing that is keeping you from doing what you really want to do? Identify it and deal with it. If it's fear, face it head on and move forward. If it's indifference, adjust your attitude and determine if you really want to do it or not. If it's self confidence, practice and work until you get better and you begin to build confidence.

Trey Wood was born with only one arm. Most people assumed that his handicap would prevent him from participating in a sport like football. Instead of feeling sorry for himself, Trey decided to prove the experts wrong. Not only did he learn to play football, he received an athletic scholarship to Sam Houston State University. He went beyond expectations and earned a starting position as a defensive back. One of his responsibilities was to knock down passes when the football was thrown in his area.

Another one-handed young man named DaWuan Miller also had a dream to play football. Miller was born without a left hand. When people would ask what happened to his left hand he would spout off, "I bit it off." In spite of his disability he, too, earned a scholarship and became the starting defensive back for Boise State University.

Both players made first team. Both excelled at their positions. Despite lacking an arm, Wood broke the career record for Sam Houston State with eleven blocked kicks. DaWuan silenced the doubters by using his one hand to intercept two passes in playoff games.

On September 16, 1995, Sam Houston State played Boise State in football. For the first time in the history of the sport, two colleges played a game with one-armed defensive backs starting for each team. Few will remember the score of the game, but no one who was there will forget how two one-armed, one-handed players' gutsy performances overshadowed the rest of the talent on the field. Each of these two football players did more with one arm than most people do with two. How did they do it? They were disciplined. They decided they wanted to, flipped the switch, and were determined.

BOW YOUR HEAD

Dear God,

Today I draw a circle around myself and ask You to search my heart. I want to run the race, live my life, and play the game in such a way as to receive the prize. Give me the discipline I need to accomplish these goals.

In Jesus' Name, Amen.

FOCUS

I'll never forget my junior season in high school. We were to play Blountstown, Florida for homecoming. Blountstown had a really good team and we knew we were going to have our hands full. They had a tailback named Fernando Jackson that ended up going to the University of Florida. Fernando had run over every opponent they had played so far.

Like any other school at homecoming there were lots of distractions during the week. There was a parade, a pep rally, and all kinds of things going on in the community. With all of the distractions, our practices during that week lacked focus. It seemed like our minds were on everything else but Blountstown.

Finally Friday night rolled around. You could tell that we were not focused at all. By the time the clock expired at the end of the fourth quarter, the score was Blountstown 52-Graceville 14. I'll never forget what Coach Kindig told us just before we got off the bus at the field house. He said, "Twenty years from now you will not remember which girl you danced with at the homecoming dance, but you will remember that you got your tails' kicked by Blountstown 52-14." He was right. I can't even remember if I went to the dance that night, but I still remember number 42 running over, around, and away from us all night long.

Bo Jackson says, "Set your goals high, and don't stop till you get there." Focus, in sports and in life, is important. If you don't learn to focus, you will never achieve your goals.

The writer of the book of Hebrews gives some insight into focusing in Hebrews 12:1-2.

"Therefore, since we have so great a cloud of witnesses surrounding us, let us also lay aside every encumbrance and the sin which so easily entangles us, and let us run with endurance the race that is set before us, fixing our eyes on Jesus, the author and perfecter of faith, who for the joy set before Him endured the cross, despising the shame, and has

sat down at the right hand of the throne of God." (Hebrews 12:1-2, NASB)

FOCUS. There are three things about focus that will help you in the game and in life.

Focus Involves Remembering Your Audience

The Bible says that we are surrounded by *"so great a cloud of witnesses."* These witnesses are those who have passed away and belong to the Lord. The word "witness" tells us two things. First, they are watching us or witnessing us. They can see what we do and how we live our lives. In other words, they take notice of the good and the bad. Secondly, it tells us they are saying something to us or witnessing to us. They are cheering us on and encouraging us in the faith.

I don't know about you, but that really is a sense of encouragement to me. I love knowing that all the saints of old and my family that has passed are cheering me on in this life. This makes me want to be the best and do the best that I can.

> *"Set your goals high and don't stop till you get there."*
>
> *Bo Jackson*

The next time you hit the field to play, the stands are going to be filled with family, friends, and fans. Keep your focus! Remember the audience is there for you. They will cheer for you, encourage you, and support you. That should make you want to give your very best effort.

Focus Includes Removing Any Obstacles

There will always be obstacles regardless of what you do. In your personal life, spiritual life, and your athletic life there will always be something or someone who is trying to keep you from accomplishing your goals.

The Bible says to *"lay aside every encumbrance and the sin which so easily entangles us ..."* These distractions can cause us to lose our focus. When a runner is running a race his focus should be on the finish line and not anything else.

Show me someone who has accomplished something great and I'll show you someone who has overcome adversity. Life is 10% what happens to you and 90% how you respond to it.

Football is a lot like life. It's a constant battle. Your teammates are going to be there for you. The coaches are going to be there for you. The crowd is going to be there for you. Focus on the goal and remove any obstacles that stand in the way of achieving it.

Focus Implies Asking the W.I.N. Question

The W.I.N. question is, "What's Important Now?" People of focus have the ability to prioritize what is happening and know what is most important.

In life and on the field there will be times when you have to ask this question. It may mean making some tough decisions about what you do for living, what you do for your family or what you do for yourself. Once you identify what "it" is, you focus and do what is necessary to meet the need.

The next time you walk on the field, you need to be asking the W.I.N. question—"What's Important Now?" You will need to ask it throughout the game, after every play, and with every possession. If you will ask this question and do what has to be done, you will not lose focus.

BOW YOUR HEAD

Dear God,

I thank You for this great opportunity that we have to play this game. You have given me the skill, the speed and the strength to play. Keep me focused and let me do my very best.

I pray that You will not allow me to become distracted from my goal. If adversity should come my way, help me to respond in a way that honors You.

In Jesus' Name, Amen.

CONFIDENCE

Confidence plays a huge role in any endeavor you embark on. If you don't believe me, ask Tiger Woods. Only a few years ago Tiger was on top of the golfing world. He had won the U.S. Open and the Australian Open when disaster hit. In a matter of hours, little did he realize life as he had known it would never be the same again. After a late night automobile accident outside of his home in Orlando, Florida it would be revealed that he had several sordid affairs with women all over the country. In the

> *"Confidence is a lot of this game or any game. If you don't think you can, you won't."*
>
> Jerry West

months that followed, his marriage fell apart, he lost many of his sponsors and millions of dollars.

After taking some time off from golf to try and salvage his marriage and refocus, he came back to the tour and tried to begin the process of rebuilding. However, it was much harder than he thought. Distracted by his divorce, injuries, and lack of playing time, his confidence took a major blow. His swagger was gone and for the first time since becoming a professional he appeared to be average. He dropped from being the number one ranked player in the world to number fifty, and it took two years to get back in the winner's column. Never underestimate the impact of confidence. When you have it, you feel like you can conqueror the world. When you lose it, it's extremely hard to rediscover.

Basketball great Jerry West says, "Confidence is a lot of this game or any game. If you don't think you can, you won't." So how do you tap into the confidence you need to be a successful person or team? I like the way the Apostle Paul addressed this issue in Philippians 4:13.

"I can do all things through Him who strengthens me." (Philippians 4:13, NASB)

CONFIDENCE. Confidence is important as a person and a team.

Confidence Begins With You

Paul says, *"I can do…"* Confidence begins with you. If you believe you can, you will. If you don't believe you can, you won't. What you believe about yourself and your abilities will dictate how you perform. Do you believe you can make the play in the clutch? Do you have the confidence that you can execute at a high level? It's called a "can do" attitude.

People of confidence don't make excuses. They do whatever they have to do to get the job done. They give maximum effort and are willing to sacrifice to be the best. They are not affected by what others say. They are self-motivated and they have an inner drive and compulsion to do what needs to be accomplished.

Confidence Affects Your Total Life

Notice the very next words in the verse, *"I can do **all things…** "* You know what all things means don't you? It means "all things."

A great example of this was a game Mary Persons

High School played against Perry High School in 2010. Through three quarters they struggled. They were down by two touchdowns in the fourth quarter. The team kept playing and refused to quit. They tied the game in the closing seconds and won it in overtime with a goal line stand! They learned from a couple of early losses that season and finished well.

Victory has a way of building confidence. When we do things right and do things well it gives us momentum. You should go into the game with all kinds of confidence. You should build your confidence and be like a springboard giving you momentum into the remainder of the season.

Don't miss this truth: confidence affects your *total* life. There is life outside of football. There is your education and your future. There will come a day when you will have a family, a job, and responsibilities that you haven't even begun to think about. Your confidence will shape your future and have an impact on your success.

Confidence Comes From Within

"*I can do all things* **through Christ who strengthens me**." If you want to know the secret to real confidence, there it is. The secret to confidence is

Christ. When you commit yourself to Christ you find the assurance that He controls your future, He is guiding your life, and that He has and will equip you for what lies ahead.

Because of Christ, you can believe in yourself. The one who possesses all power and ability lives in your heart. You can be confident because He will be with you in the battles of life and He will never leave you.

Right now football is important for you. You have set a goal. You have worked hard, and you are about to walk out on the field of battle. Your brothers will be with you and Christ is for you. The Bible tells us, "If Christ is for us, who shall stand against us?" That should give you all the confidence you need.

BOW YOUR HEAD

Dear God,

I thank You for the confidence I find in You. I pray that as I play that I will have a "can do" attitude on the field. May my actions and attitudes reflect the fact that I belong to You and that You are the source of my strength.

In Jesus' Name, Amen.

DETERMINATION

Several years ago Shug Jordan, head football coach at Auburn University, asked one of his former players, Mike Kollin, who was then playing linebacker for the Miami Dolphins, if he would help his alma mater do some recruiting of football players. Kollin agreed: "Sure, coach, what kind of player are you looking for?"

Coach Jordan said, "Well Mike, you know there's that guy who when you knock him down, just stays down?" Kollin answered, "We don't want him, do we coach?"

"You're right about that. Then there's that guy who, when you knock him down, gets up. But when you knock him down again, then he stays down." Kollin said, "We don't want him either, do we coach?"

"No, Mike, we don't. But then there is that guy, you knock him down, he gets right back up. You knock him down again, he gets up. You knock him down again and he gets up again." Kollin said, "Now that's the guy we want, right coach?"

"No," said Coach Jordan. "We don't want him either. What I want is for you to find me the guy who keeps knocking everyone down. That's the guy we want!"

There is an old Chinese proverb which says, "Fall down seven times, get up eight." People of determination are the kind of people who weather the storms of life well because they are determined to do so. They are the people who put in the extra work, and give the extra effort to be the best at what they do. Athletes who are determined are the people that get that extra yard, make the catch, make the throw, make that open field tackle, and make the key block when the game is on the line.

The Bible gives us a snapshot of what it means to be determined in Ephesians 6.

"Therefore, take up the full armor of God, so that you will be able to resist in the evil day, and having done everything, to

stand firm." (Ephesians 6:13, NASB)

DETERMINATION. Here are three things that will help you to measure your determination:

You Focus On the Task

The first part of the sixth chapter of Ephesians is all about putting on the armor of God. Paul uses an analogy of a soldier suiting up for battle. This soldier understands that he's about to go into battle, so he's getting ready for what is to come. He is focused on the task before him.

I know you understand that you are going into battle. Just like this soldier, you are a warrior. The battle field is a stadium and the task is to defeat your opponent. In order to win a victory you must focus on the task. Remember this: "You can't depend on your eyes when your mind is out of focus." You've never truly focused unless you are mentally engaged.

You Are Familiar with Your Adversary

Spiritually we have an adversary whose agenda is to kill, steal, and destroy. The devil wants to kill your joy, steal your peace, and destroy your testimony. We all know the struggle between good and evil.

You had better believe that this soldier who is getting dressed for battle knew his enemy. He knew his strengths and his weaknesses. He knew his tendencies and his techniques. This soldier knew everything there was to know about his enemy. He had studied him and was very familiar with the way he fought and had put together a battle plan that would hopefully lead to victory.

You know your opponent. They are a good football team. They have speed and they are athletic. You've seen them on tape. You know what their strengths are and where they are vulnerable. It's time to go and play with determination and make a statement. The difference between great teams and mediocre teams is that great teams step up and execute and make a statement.

You Finish Your Preparation

This soldier in Ephesians 6 put each piece of armor on intentionally. This armor had no covering in the back. In other words, after the preparation was done he was determined to face his adversary head on. There was no plan for retreat.

You have worked hard. You've studied, practice and prepared to the best of your ability. The coaches have put together the game plan. You know what you're up against. You have done everything to stand on the field. So stand—make a statement and exercise your determination! Don't quit, back up, back down or retreat! Go and finish the preparation and win a great victory!

BOW YOUR HEAD

Dear God,

I thank You for the confidence I find in You. I pray that as I play that I will have a "can do" attitude on the field. May my actions and attitudes reflect the fact that I belong to You and that You are the source of my strength.

In Jesus' Name, Amen.

Me and Coach Rodney Walker,
GACA 2014 Hall of Fame Nominee.

"The Kick" that won the Cairo Game
and sent Mary Persons to the Quarter Finals in 2012.

With Brian Nelson,
Head Coach,
Mary Persons
High School,
Forsyth Georgia.

With Jeremy Rayburn,
Offensive Coordinator.

My son, Micah.

Micah (#85) played Wide Receiver
for the Bulldogs.

Me on the sideline.

Friday night in Forsyth, Georgia.

Micah held for field goals and extra points.

"Senior Night 2012."

"The Twins." Megan and Micah, Mary Persons Homecoming 2012.

Made in the USA
Lexington, KY
26 September 2014